pause & reflect

MEDITATIONS FOR FAMILIES

pause & reflect

MEDITATIONS FOR FAMILIES

ONE VOICE
PRESS

WILMETTE, ILLINOIS

One Voice Press
401 Greenleaf Avenue
Wilmette, Illinois 60091

Printed in the United States of America on
acid-free paper ∞

23 22 21 20   4 3 2 1
ISBN: 978-1-61851-175-1

Book design by Patrick Falso
Cover design by Carlos Esparza

CONTENTS

CONTENTS

INTRODUCTION

There is much in our modern world compet-
ing for our attention. Technology is changing
at a pace so rapid that most of us cannot keep
up, let alone take the time to process the ways
in which it is affecting us. As we go about our
daily lives we are seemingly assaulted with
an endless series of distractions. The need to
retreat from the stress and chaos that so often
surrounds us, to center ourselves and reflect on
our inner reality, has never been of more vital
importance. It is with this in mind that One
Voice Press is happy to present this, the second
title in its recently launched *Pause & Reflect*
series.

Pause & Reflect is a series that presents med-
itative passages from the writings of the Bahá'í
Faith arranged around particular themes.
While the Bahá'í Faith places a great deal of
importance on meditation and the cultivation
of spirituality, it is also a religion that calls for

action and societal transformation. Meditation, from a Bahá'í perspective, is not exclusively a means for personal growth but also a tool that should equip us with insights and awareness that can be translated into action in our lives and in the communities in which we live.

Perhaps there is no more significant bridge between our individual lives and the life of our communities than the theme of this little book: families. Families, after all, are building blocks of civilization. The quality of relationships between family members influences the culture of wider society. In the arena of marriage, a couple has the opportunity to practice and embody lofty values concerning the equality of men and women, collaboration, and the education of children. As families grow spiritually, so too will humanity mature. In the words of 'Abdu'l-Bahá, "A family is a nation in miniature. . . . The conditions surrounding the family surround the nation."* How valuable, how worthy the path walked by all members of a family who seek to contribute to the betterment of the world in which they live.

---

* 'Abdu'l-Bahá, *The Promulgation of Universal Peace,* p. 217.

Yet no family is removed from the effects of larger social forces. Just as we influence our environment, it influences us. For this reason, many challenges arise for families across the globe. They are torn apart by forces of immorality, war, prejudice, and materialism, to name but a few. Young families in particular are faced with the struggles of the modern world, including shifting economies, climate change, and political discord that fractures entire populations. Under such conditions, many yearn for change, for higher degrees of harmony, for both material and spiritual advancement, for themselves and their children.

The passages collected here touch on such subjects as the unique bond between wife and husband, the raising of children and the sacred obligation to educate them, and the vitality of the family as a whole. The words on these pages orient us, above all, toward love and unity, toward equality and cooperation, and toward spiritual growth. It is hoped that this book will offer opportunities for reflection and discussion within the homes of families wishing to explore the nature of their lives and relationships.

Marriage:
The Bond between
Husband and Wife

BAHÁ'U'LLÁH

1

Enter ye into wedlock, that after you another may arise in your stead.

2

Living in seclusion or practicing asceticism is not acceptable in the presence of God. It behooveth them that are endued with insight and understanding to observe that which will cause joy and radiance. . . . Deprive not yourselves of the bounties which have been created for your sake.

3

Women and men have been and will always be equal in the sight of God. The Dawning-Place of the Light of God sheddeth its radiance upon all with the same effulgence. Verily God created women for men, and men for women.

'ABDU'L-BAHÁ

4

Bahá'í marriage is the commitment of the two parties one to the other, and their mutual attachment of mind and heart. Each must, however, exercise the utmost care to become thoroughly acquainted with the character of the other, that the binding covenant between them may be a tie that will endure forever. Their purpose must be this: to become loving companions and comrades and at one with each other for time and eternity.

5

The true marriage of Bahá'ís is this, that husband and wife should be united both physically and spiritually, that they may ever improve the spiritual life of each other, and may enjoy everlasting unity throughout all the worlds of God.

6

In Thine almighty wisdom Thou hast enjoined marriage upon the peoples, that the generations of men may succeed one another in this contingent world, and that ever, so long as the world shall last, they may busy themselves at the Threshold of Thy oneness with servitude and worship, with salutation, adoration and praise.

7

The love between husband and wife should not be purely physical, nay rather it must be spiritual and heavenly. These two souls should be considered as one soul. How difficult it would be to divide a single soul! Nay, great would be the difficulty!

8

. . . marriage must be a union of the body and of the spirit as well, for here both husband and wife are aglow with the same wine, both are enamored of the same matchless Face, both live and move through the same spirit, both are illumined by the same glory. This connection between them is a spiritual one, hence it is a bond that will abide forever. Likewise do they enjoy strong and lasting ties in the physical world as well, for if the marriage is based both on the spirit and the body, that union is a true one, hence it will endure. If, however, the bond is physical and nothing more, it is sure to be only temporary, and must inexorably end in separation.

9

When, therefore, the people of Bahá undertake to marry, the union must be a true relationship, a spiritual coming together as well as a physical one, so that throughout every phase of life, and in all the worlds of God, their union will endure; for this real oneness is a gleaming out of the love of God.

10

The Lord, peerless is He, hath made woman and man to abide with each other in the closest companionship, and to be even as a single soul. They are two helpmates, two intimate friends, who should be concerned about the welfare of each other.

11

The world of humanity has two wings, as it were: One is the female; the other is the male. If one wing be defective, the strong perfect wing will not be capable of flight. The world of humanity has two hands. If one be imperfect, the capable hand is restricted and unable to perform its duties.

12

And let it be known once more that until woman and man recognize and realize equality, social and political progress here or anywhere will not be possible. . . . Until these two members are equal in strength, the oneness of humanity cannot be established, and the happiness and felicity of mankind will not be a reality.

13

The happiness of mankind will be realized when women and men coordinate and advance equally, for each is the complement and helpmeet of the other.

14

In short, the foundation of the Kingdom of God is based upon harmony and love, oneness, relationship and union, not upon differences, especially between husband and wife.

SHOGHI EFFENDI

15

The Bahá'í Teachings do not only encourage marital life, considering it the natural and normal way of existence for every sane, healthy and socially-conscious and responsible person, but raise marriage to the status of a Divine institution, its chief and sacred purpose being the perpetuation of the human race—which is the very flower of the entire creation—and its elevation to the true station destined for it by God.

16

That two people should live their lives in love and harmony is of far greater importance than that they should be consumed with passion for each other. The one is a great rock of strength on which to lean in time of need; the other a purely temporary thing which may at any time die out.

17

Bahá'u'lláh has clearly stated the consent of all living parents is required for a Bahá'í marriage. This applies whether the parents are Bahá'ís or non-Bahá'ís, divorced for years or not. This great law He has laid down to strengthen the social fabric, to knit closer the ties of the home, to place a certain gratitude and respect in the hearts of children for those who have given them life and sent their souls out on the eternal journey towards their Creator.

THE UNIVERSAL
HOUSE OF JUSTICE

18

There are . . . times when a wife should defer to her husband, and times when a husband should defer to his wife, but neither should ever unjustly dominate the other.

19

A couple should study each other's character and spend time getting to know each
other before they decide to marry, and when
they do marry it should be with the intention
of establishing an eternal bond.

20

Freedom of movement and availability of time enable many youth to serve in ways that are directly related to the needs of the community, but as they advance further into their twenties, their horizons broaden. Other dimensions of a coherent life, equally demanding and highly meritorious, begin to make stronger claims on their attention. For many, an immediate priority will be further education, academic or vocational, according to the possibilities before them, and new spaces for interaction with society open up. Moreover, young women and men become acutely conscious of the exhortations of the Supreme Pen to "enter into wedlock" that they may "bring forth one who will make mention of Me amid My servants" and to "engage in crafts and professions." Having taken up an occupation, youth naturally try to contribute to their field . . . they strive to be examples of integrity and excellence in their work. Bahá'u'lláh extols those "that earn a livelihood by their calling and spend upon themselves and upon their kindred for the love of God, the Lord of all worlds." This generation of youth will form families that secure the foundations of flourishing communities.

Children and
Parenting

BAHÁ'U'LLÁH

1

Show honor to your parents and pay homage to them. This will cause blessings to descend upon you from the clouds of the bounty of your Lord, the Exalted, the Great.

'ABDU'L-BAHÁ

2

It is highly important for man to raise a family. So long as he is young, because of youthful self-complacency, he does not realize its significance, but this will be a source of regret when he grows old.

3

Ye should consider the question of goodly character as of the first importance. It is incumbent upon every father and mother to counsel their children over a long period, and guide them unto those things which lead to everlasting honor.

4

In this new and wondrous Age, the unshakeable foundation is the teaching of sciences and arts . . . every child must be taught crafts and arts, to the degree that is needful.

5

Training in morals and good conduct is far more important than book learning. A child that is cleanly, agreeable, of good character, well-behaved—even though he be ignorant—is preferable to a child that is rude, unwashed, ill-natured, and yet becoming deeply versed in all the sciences and arts. The reason for this is that the child who conducts himself well, even though he be ignorant, is of benefit to others, while an ill-natured, ill-behaved child is corrupted and harmful to others, even though he be learned. If, however, the child be trained to be both learned and good, the result is light upon light.

6

Children are even as a branch that is fresh and green; they will grow up in whatever way ye train them. Take the utmost care to give them high ideals and goals, so that once they come of age, they will cast their beams like brilliant candles on the world, and will not be defiled by lusts and passions in the way of animals, heedless and unaware, but instead will set their hearts on achieving everlasting honor and acquiring all the excellences of humankind.

7

Our meaning is that qualities of the spirit are the basic and divine foundation, and adorn the true essence of man; and knowledge is the cause of human progress. The beloved of God must attach great importance to this matter, and carry it forward with enthusiasm and zeal.

8

O ye loving mothers, know ye that in God's
sight, the best of all ways to worship Him
is to educate the children and train them in all
the perfections of humankind; and no nobler
deed than this can be imagined.

9

Furthermore, the education of woman is more necessary and important than that of man, for woman is the trainer of the child from its infancy . . . for it is the mother who rears, nurtures and guides the growth of the child. . . . If the educator be incompetent, the educated will be correspondingly lacking. This is evident and incontrovertible. Could the student be brilliant and accomplished if the teacher is illiterate and ignorant? The mothers are the first educators of mankind; if they be imperfect, alas for the condition and future of the race.

10

These children are even as young plants, and teaching them the prayers is as letting the rain pour down upon them, that they may wax tender and fresh, and the soft breezes of the love of God may blow over them, making them to tremble with joy.

11

As to thy question regarding the education of children: it behooveth thee to nurture them at the breast of the love of God, and urge them onward to the things of the spirit, that they may turn their faces unto God; that their ways may conform to the rules of good conduct and their character be second to none; that they make their own all the graces and praiseworthy qualities of humankind; acquire a sound knowledge of the various branches of learning, so that from the very beginning of life they may become spiritual beings, dwellers in the Kingdom, enamored of the sweet breaths of holiness, and may receive an education religious, spiritual, and of the Heavenly Realm.

12

Let the mothers consider that whatever concerneth the education of children is of the first importance. Let them put forth every effort in this regard, for when the bough is green and tender it will grow in whatever way ye train it. Therefore is it incumbent upon the mothers to rear their little ones even as a gardener tendeth his young plants.

13

In this new and wondrous Age, the unshakable foundation is the teaching of sciences and arts. According to explicit Holy Texts, every child must be taught crafts and arts, to the degree that is needful. Wherefore, in every city and village, schools must be established and every child in that city or village is to engage in study to the necessary degree.

14

While the children are yet in their infancy feed them from the breast of heavenly grace, foster them in the cradle of all excellence, rear them in the embrace of bounty. Give them the advantage of every useful kind of knowledge. Let them share in every new and rare and wondrous craft and art. Bring them up to work and strive, and accustom them to hardship. Teach them to dedicate their lives to matters of great import, and inspire them to undertake studies that will benefit mankind.

15

The education and training of children is among the most meritorious acts of humankind and draweth down the grace and favor of the All-Merciful, for education is the indispensable foundation of all human excellence and alloweth man to work his way to the heights of abiding glory.

16

If a child be trained from his infancy, he will, through the loving care of the Holy Gardener, drink in the crystal waters of the spirit and of knowledge, like a young tree amid the rilling brooks. And certainly he will gather to himself the bright rays of the Sun of Truth, and through its light and heat will grow ever fresh and fair in the garden of life.

17

Every child is potentially the light of the world—and at the same time its darkness; wherefore must the question of education be accounted as of primary importance. From his infancy, the child must be nursed at the breast of God's love, and nurtured in the embrace of His knowledge, that he may radiate light, grow in spirituality, be filled with wisdom and learning, and take on the characteristics of the angelic host.

18

Children must be most carefully watched over, protected and trained; in such consisteth true parenthood and parental mercy.

19

For mothers are the first educators, the first mentors; and truly it is the mothers who determine the happiness, the future greatness, the courteous ways and learning and judgement, the understanding and the faith of their little ones.

20

Among the greatest of all services that can possibly be rendered by man to Almighty God is the education and training of children, young plants of the Abhá Paradise, so that these children, fostered by grace in the way of salvation, growing like pearls of divine bounty in the shell of education, will one day bejewel the crown of abiding glory.

21

Thus the husband and wife are brought into affinity, are united and harmonized, even as though they were one person. Through their mutual union, companionship and love great results are produced in the world, both material and spiritual. The spiritual result is the appearance of divine bounties. The material result is the children who are born in the cradle of the love of God, who are nurtured by the breast of the knowledge of God, who are brought up in the bosom of the gift of God, and who are fostered in the lap of the training of God.

22

The child must not be oppressed or censured because it is undeveloped; it must be patiently trained.

23

It is for this reason that, in this new cycle, education and training are recorded in the Book of God as obligatory and not voluntary. That is, it is enjoined upon the father and mother, as a duty, to strive with all effort to train the daughter and the son, to nurse them from the breast of knowledge and to rear them in the bosom of sciences and arts.

24

Likewise, parents endure the greatest toil and trouble for their children, and often, by the time the latter have reached the age of maturity, the former have hastened to the world beyond. Rarely do the mother and father enjoy in this world the rewards of all the pain and trouble they have endured for their children. The children must therefore, in return for this pain and trouble, make charitable contributions and perform good works in their name, and implore pardon and forgiveness for their souls. You should therefore, in return for the love and kindness of your father, give to the poor in his name and, with the utmost lowliness and fervour, pray for God's pardon and forgiveness and seek His infinite mercy.

SHOGHI EFFENDI

25

A God that is only loving or only just is not a perfect God. The Divinity has to possess both of these aspects as every father ought to express both in his attitude towards his children. If we ponder a while, we will see that our welfare can be ensured only when both of these divine attributes are equally emphasized and practiced.

THE UNIVERSAL
HOUSE OF JUSTICE

26

Independent of the level of their education, parents are in a critical position to shape the spiritual development of their children. They should not ever underestimate their capacity to mold their children's moral character. For they exercise indispensable influence through the home environment they consciously create by their love of God, their striving to adhere to His laws, their spirit of service to His Cause, their lack of fanaticism, and their freedom from the corrosive effects of backbiting.

27

Children are the most precious treasure a community can possess, for in them are the promise and guarantee of the future. They bear the seeds of the character of future society which is largely shaped by what the adults constituting the community do or fail to do with respect to children. They are a trust no community can neglect with impunity. An all-embracing love of children, the manner of treating them, the quality of the attention shown them, the spirit of adult behavior toward them—these are all among the vital aspects of the requisite attitude. Love demands discipline, the courage to accustom children to hardship, not to indulge their whims or leave them entirely to their own devices. An atmosphere needs to be maintained in which children feel that they belong to the community and share in its purpose.

Family Relationships

BAHÁ'U'LLÁH

1

The beginning of magnanimity is when man expendeth his wealth on himself, on his family and on the poor among his brethren in his Faith.

2

Trustworthiness is the greatest portal leading unto the tranquility and security of the people. In truth the stability of every affair hath depended and doth depend upon it. All the domains of power, of grandeur and of wealth are illumined by its light.

3

Lay not on any soul a load which ye would not wish to be laid upon you, and desire not for any one the things ye would not desire for yourselves.

4

Do not busy yourselves in your own concerns; let your thoughts be fixed upon that which will rehabilitate the fortunes of mankind and sanctify the hearts and souls of men. This can best be achieved through pure and holy deeds, through a virtuous life and a goodly behavior.

5

Should prosperity befall thee, rejoice not, and should abasement come upon thee, grieve not, for both shall pass away and be no more.

6

With the utmost friendliness and in a spirit of perfect fellowship take ye counsel together, and dedicate the precious days of your lives to the betterment of the world.

7

Be ye as the fingers of one hand, the members of one body.

'ABDU'L-BAHÁ

8

If love and agreement are manifest in a single family, that family will advance, become illumined and spiritual; but if enmity and hatred exist within it destruction and dispersion are inevitable.

9

A family is a nation in miniature. Simply enlarge the circle of the household and you have the nation. Enlarge the circle of nations and you have all humanity. The conditions surrounding the family surround the nation.

10

In this glorious Cause the life of a married couple should resemble the life of the angels in heaven—a life full of joy and spiritual delight, a life of unity and concord, a friendship both mental and physical. The home should be orderly and well-organized. Their ideas and thoughts should be like the rays of the sun of truth and the radiance of the brilliant stars in the heavens. Even as two birds they should warble melodies upon the branches of the tree of fellowship and harmony. They should always be elated with joy and gladness and be a source of happiness to the hearts of others. They should set an example to their fellow-men, manifest true and sincere love towards each other and educate their children in such a manner as to blazon the fame and glory of their family.

11

The integrity of the family bond must be constantly considered, and the rights of the individual members must not be transgressed. . . . All these rights and prerogatives must be conserved, yet the unity of the family must be sustained. The injury of one shall be considered the injury of all; the comfort of each, the comfort of all; the honor of one, the honor of all.

12

According to the teachings of Bahá'u'lláh the family, being a human unit, must be educated according to the rules of sanctity. All the virtues must be taught the family.

13

Man must consult in all things for this will lead him to the depths of each problem and enable him to find the right solution.

14

Therefore, love humanity with all your heart and soul. If you meet a poor man, assist him; if you see the sick, heal him; reassure the affrighted one, render the cowardly noble and courageous, educate the ignorant, associate with the stranger. Emulate God. Consider how kindly, how lovingly He deals with all, and follow His example. You must treat people in accordance with the divine precepts—in other words, treat them as kindly as God treats them, for this is the greatest attainment possible for the world of humanity.

15

Every imperfect soul is self-centered and thinketh only of his own good. But as his thoughts expand a little he will begin to think of the welfare and comfort of his family. If his ideas still more widen, his concern will be the felicity of his fellow citizens; and if still they widen, he will be thinking of the glory of his land and of his race. But when ideas and views reach the utmost degree of expansion and attain the stage of perfection, then will he be interested in the exaltation of humankind.

16

Act in such a way that your heart may be free from hatred. Let not your heart be offended with anyone. If someone commits an error and wrong toward you, you must instantly forgive him.

17

Do not complain of others. Refrain from reprimanding them, and if you wish to give admonition or advice, let it be offered in such a way that it will not burden the bearer. Turn all your thoughts toward bringing joy to hearts.

18

Beware! Beware! lest ye offend any heart. Assist the world of humanity as much as possible. Be the source of consolation to every sad one, assist every weak one, be helpful to every indigent one, care for every sick one, be the cause of glorification to every lowly one, and shelter those who are overshadowed by fear.

19

It is indeed a good and praiseworthy thing to progress materially, but in so doing, let us not neglect the more important spiritual progress.

20

Do not be satisfied until each one with whom you are concerned is to you as a member of your family. Regard each one either as a father, or as a brother, or as a sister, or as a mother, or as a child. If you can attain to this, your difficulties will vanish, you will know what to do.

21

. . . consultation must have for its object the investigation of truth. He who expresses an opinion should not voice it as correct and right but set it forth as a contribution to the consensus of opinion, for the light of reality becomes apparent when two opinions coincide. . . . Man should weigh his opinions with the utmost serenity, calmness and composure. Before expressing his own views he should carefully consider the views already advanced by others. If he finds that a previously expressed opinion is more true and worthy, he should accept it immediately and not willfully hold to an opinion of his own. By this excellent method he endeavors to arrive at unity and truth. . . .

22

. . . true consultation is spiritual conference in the attitude and atmosphere of love. Members must love each other in the spirit of fellowship in order that good results may be forthcoming. Love and fellowship are the foundation.

23

They have not properly understood that man's supreme honor and real happiness lie in self-respect, in high resolves and noble purposes, in integrity and moral quality, in immaculacy of mind. They have, rather, imagined that their greatness consists in the accumulation, by whatever means may offer, of worldly goods.

24

Beware lest ye harm any soul, or make any heart to sorrow; lest ye wound any man with your words, be he known to you or a stranger, be he friend or foe. Pray ye for all; ask ye that all be blessed, all be forgiven.

25

When you love a member of your family or a compatriot, let it be with a ray of the Infinite Love! Let it be in God, and for God! Wherever you find the attributes of God love that person, whether he be of your family or of another.

26

Consider the harmful effect of discord and dissension in a family; then reflect upon the favors and blessings which descend upon that family when unity exists among its various members. What incalculable benefits and blessings would descend upon the great human family if unity and brotherhood were established!

27

Note ye how easily, where unity existeth in a given family, the affairs of that family are conducted; what progress the members of that family make, how they prosper in the world. Their concerns are in order, they enjoy comfort and tranquility, they are secure, their position is assured, they come to be envied by all. Such a family but addeth to its stature and its lasting honor, as day succeedeth day.

SHOGHI EFFENDI

28

Deep as are family ties, we must always remember that the spiritual ties are far deeper; they are everlasting and survive death, whereas physical ties, unless supported by spiritual bonds, are confined to this life.

29

We cannot segregate the human heart from the environment outside us and say that once one of these is reformed everything will be improved. Man is organic with the world. His inner life moulds the environment and is itself also deeply affected by it. The one acts upon the other and every abiding change in the life of man is the result of these mutual reactions.

THE UNIVERSAL
HOUSE OF JUSTICE

30

A Bahá'í who has a problem may wish to make his own decision upon it after prayer and after weighing all the aspects of it in his own mind; he may prefer to seek the counsel of individual friends or of professional counsellors such as his doctor or lawyer so that he can consider such advice when making his decision; or in a case where several people are involved, such as a family situation, he may want to gather together those who are affected so that they may arrive at a collective decision.

31

. . . there is a much wider sphere of relationships between men and women than in the home, and this too we should consider in the context of Bahá'í society, not in that of past or present social norms. For example, although the mother is the first educator of the child, and the most important formative influence in his development, the father also has the responsibility of educating his children, and this responsibility is so weighty that Bahá'u'lláh has stated that a father who fails to exercise it forfeits his rights of fatherhood.

Similarly, although the primary responsibility for supporting the family financially is placed upon the husband, this does not by any means imply that the place of woman is confined to the home.

Home

BAHÁ'U'LLÁH

1

Blessed is the spot wherein the anthem of His praise is raised, and blessed the ear that hearkeneth unto that which hath been sent down from the heaven of the loving-kindness of thy Lord, the All-Merciful.

2

O friend, the heart is the dwelling-place of eternal mysteries: Make it not the home of fleeting fancies. Waste not the treasure of thy precious life occupied with this swiftly passing world. Thou comest from the world of holiness: Bind not thine heart to the earth. Thou art a dweller in the court of reunion: Choose not the homeland of the dust.

'ABDU'L-BAHÁ

3

Know thou of a certainty that every house wherein the anthem of praise is raised to the Realm of Glory in celebration of the Name of God is indeed a heavenly home, and one of the gardens of delight in the Paradise of God.

4

This earth is one home and native land. God has created mankind with equal endowment and right to live upon the earth. As a city is the home of all its inhabitants although each may have his individual place of residence therein, so the earth's surface is one wide native land or home for all races of humankind.

5

This is a spiritual house, the home of the spirit. There is no discord here; all is love and unity. When souls are gathered together in this way, the divine bestowals descend.

6

This is in truth a Bahá'í house. Every time such a house or meeting place is founded it becomes one of the greatest aids to the general development of the town and country to which it belongs. It encourages the growth of learning and science and is known for its intense spirituality and for the love it spreads among the peoples.

7

The upbuilding of a home, the bringing of joy and comfort into human hearts are truly glories of mankind.

8

The whole earth is one home, and all peoples, did they but know it, are bathed in the oneness of God's mercy. God created all. He gives sustenance to all. He guides and trains all under the shadow of His bounty. We must follow the example God Himself gives us, and do away with all disputations and quarrels.

9

The surface of the earth is one home; humanity is one family and household. Distinctions and boundaries are artificial, human. Why should there be discord and strife among men? All must become united and coordinated in service to the world of humanity.

10

My home is the home of peace. My home is the home of joy and delight. My home is the home of laughter and exultation. Whosoever enters through the portals of this home, must go out with gladsome heart. This is the home of light; whosoever enters here must become illumined. This is the home of knowledge: the one who enters it must receive knowledge. This is the home of love: those who come in must learn the lessons of love; thus may they know how to love each other.

Love and Unity

BAHÁ'U'LLÁH

1

A pure heart is as a mirror; cleanse it with the burnish of love and severance from all save God, that the true sun may shine within it and the eternal morning dawn.

2

Blessed is he who preferreth his brother before himself.

3

Ye are the fruits of one tree, and the leaves of one branch. Deal ye one with another with the utmost love and harmony, with friendliness and fellowship.

4

All men have been created to carry forward an ever-advancing civilization. The Almighty beareth Me witness: To act like the beasts of the field is unworthy of man. Those virtues that befit his dignity are forbearance, mercy, compassion and loving-kindness towards all the peoples and kindreds of the earth.

'ABDU'L-BAHÁ

5

Love is the most great law that ruleth this mighty and heavenly cycle, the unique power that bindeth together the divers elements of this material world, the supreme magnetic force that directeth the movements of the spheres in the celestial realms. Love revealeth with unfailing and limitless power the mysteries latent in the universe.

6

. . . for love is light, no matter in what abode it dwelleth; and hate is darkness, no matter where it may make its nest. O friends of God! That the hidden Mystery may stand revealed, and the secret essence of all things may be disclosed, strive ye to banish that darkness for ever and ever.

7

The source of perfect unity and love in the world of existence is the bond and one-ness of reality. When the divine and funda-mental reality enters human hearts and lives, it conserves and protects all states and conditions of mankind, establishing that intrinsic oneness of the world of humanity which can only come into being through the efficacy of the Holy Spirit. For the Holy Spirit is like unto the life in the human body, which blends all differences of parts and members in unity and agreement.

8

Be in perfect unity. Never become angry with one another. Let your eyes be directed toward the kingdom of truth and not toward the world of creation. Love the creatures for the sake of God and not for themselves. You will never become angry or impatient if you love them for the sake of God.

9

Humanity is not perfect. There are imperfections in every human being, and you will always become unhappy if you look toward the people themselves. But if you look toward God, you will love them and be kind to them, for the world of God is the world of perfection and complete mercy.

10

Let them purify their sight and behold all humankind as leaves and blossoms and fruits of the tree of being. Let them at all times concern themselves with doing a kindly thing for one of their fellows, offering to someone love, consideration, thoughtful help. Let them see no one as their enemy, or as wishing them ill, but think of all humankind as their friends; regarding the alien as an intimate, the stranger as a companion, staying free of prejudice, drawing no lines.

11

Reflect ye as to other than human forms of life and be ye admonished thereby: those clouds that drift apart cannot produce the bounty of the rain, and are soon lost; a flock of sheep, once scattered, falleth prey to the wolf, and birds that fly alone will be caught fast in the claws of the hawk. What greater demonstration could there be that unity leadeth to flourishing life, while dissension and withdrawing from the others, will lead only to misery; for these are the sure ways to bitter disappointment and ruin.

12

We must look higher than all earthly thoughts; detach ourselves from every material idea, crave for the things of the spirit; fix our eyes on the everlasting bountiful Mercy of the Almighty, who will fill our souls with the gladness of joyful service to His command "Love One Another."

13

Discord deprives humanity of the eternal favors of God; therefore, we must forget all imaginary causes of difference and seek the very fundamentals of the divine religions in order that we may associate in perfect love and accord and consider humankind as one family, the surface of the earth as one nationality and all races as one humanity.

14

I charge you all that each one of you concentrate all the thoughts of your heart on love and unity. When a thought of war comes, oppose it by a stronger thought of peace. A thought of hatred must be destroyed by a more powerful thought of love.

15

The diversity in the human family should be the cause of love and harmony, as it is in music where many different notes blend together in the making of a perfect chord.

16

The fact that we imagine ourselves to be right and everybody else wrong is the greatest of all obstacles in the path towards unity, and unity is necessary if we would reach truth, for truth is one.

17

For one another must ye give up even life itself. To every human being must ye be infinitely kind. Call none a stranger; think none to be your foe. Be ye as if all men were your close kin and honored friends. Walk ye in such wise that this fleeting world will change into a splendor and this dismal heap of dust become a palace of delights. Such is the counsel of 'Abdu'l-Bahá, this hapless servant.

18

. . . when you meet those whose opinions differ from your own, do not turn away your face from them. All are seeking truth, and there are many roads leading thereto. Truth has many aspects, but it remains always and forever one.

19

The first sign of faith is love. The message of the holy, divine Manifestations is love; the phenomena of creation are based upon love; the radiance of the world is due to love; the well-being and happiness of the world depend upon it. Therefore, I admonish you that you must strive throughout the human world to diffuse the light of love. The people of this world are thinking of warfare; you must be peacemakers. The nations are self-centered; you must be thoughtful of others rather than yourselves. They are neglectful; you must be mindful. They are asleep; you should be awake and alert. May each one of you be as a shining star in the horizon of eternal glory.

20

May you become as the waves of one sea, stars of the same heaven, fruits adorning the same tree, roses of one garden in order that through you the oneness of humanity may establish its temple in the world of mankind, for you are the ones who are called to uplift the cause of unity among the nations of the earth.

21

. . . the perfections of God, the divine virtues, are reflected or revealed in the human reality. Just as the light and effulgence of the sun when cast upon a polished mirror are reflected fully, gloriously, so, likewise, the qualities and attributes of Divinity are radiated from the depths of a pure human heart.

22

Wherefore must the friends of God, with utter sanctity, with one accord, rise up in the spirit, in unity with one another, to such a degree that they will become even as one being and one soul. On such a plane as this, physical bodies play no part, rather doth the spirit take over and rule; and when its power encompasseth all then is spiritual union achieved. Strive ye by day and night to cultivate your unity to the fullest degree.

23

What a power is love! It is the most wonderful, the greatest of all living powers. Love gives life to the lifeless. Love lights a flame in the heart that is cold. Love brings hope to the hopeless and gladdens the hearts of the sorrowful.

24

There are four kinds of love. The first is the love that flows from God to man; it consists of the inexhaustible graces, the Divine effulgence and heavenly illumination. Through this love the world of being receives life. Through this love man is endowed with physical existence, until, through the breath of the Holy Spirit—this same love—he receives eternal life and becomes the image of the Living God. This love is the origin of all the love in the world of creation.

The second is the love that flows from man to God. This is faith, attraction to the Divine, enkindlement, progress, entrance into the Kingdom of God, receiving the Bounties of God, illumination with the lights of the Kingdom. This love is the origin of all philanthropy; this love causes the hearts of men to reflect the rays of the Sun of Reality.

The third is the love of God towards the Self or Identity of God. This is the transfiguration of His Beauty, the reflection of Himself in the mirror of His Creation. This is the reality of love, the Ancient Love, the Eternal

Love. Through one ray of this Love all other love exists.

The fourth is the love of man for man. The love which exists between the hearts of believers is prompted by the ideal of the unity of spirits. This love is attained through the knowledge of God, so that men see the Divine Love reflected in the heart. Each sees in the other the Beauty of God reflected in the soul, and finding this point of similarity, they are attracted to one another in love. This love will make all men the waves of one sea, this love will make them all the stars of one heaven and the fruits of one tree. This love will bring the realization of true accord, the foundation of real unity.

25

. . . the love which sometimes exists between friends is not (true) love, because it is subject to transmutation; this is merely fascination. As the breeze blows, the slender trees yield. . . . This kind of love is originated by the accidental conditions of life. This is not love, it is merely acquaintanceship; it is subject to change.

26

What profit is there in agreeing that universal friendship is good, and talking of the solidarity of the human race as a grand ideal? Unless these thoughts are translated into the world of action, they are useless.

27

If I love you, I need not continually speak of my love—you will know without any words. On the other hand if I love you not, that also will you know—and you would not believe me, were I to tell you in a thousand words, that I loved you.

28

All God's prophets have brought the message of love. None has ever thought that war and hate are good. Everyone agrees in saying that love and kindness are best.

29

Love manifests its reality in deeds, not only in words—these alone are without effect. In order that love may manifest its power there must be an object, an instrument, a motive.

30

There are many ways of expressing the love principle; there is love for the family, for the country, for the race, there is political enthusiasm, there is also the love of community of interest in service. These are all ways and means of showing the power of love.

31

Love is unlimited, boundless, infinite! Material things are limited, circumscribed, finite. You cannot adequately express infinite love by limited means.

32

The perfect love needs an unselfish instrument, absolutely freed from fetters of every kind. The love of family is limited; the tie of blood relationship is not the strongest bond. Frequently members of the same family disagree, and even hate each other.

Patriotic love is finite; the love of one's country causing hatred of all others, is not perfect love! Compatriots also are not free from quarrels amongst themselves.

The love of race is limited; there is some union here, but that is insufficient. Love must be free from boundaries!

To love our own race may mean hatred of all others, and even people of the same race often dislike each other.

Political love also is much bound up with hatred of one party for another; this love is very limited and uncertain.

The love of community of interest in service is likewise fluctuating; frequently competitions arise, which lead to jealousy, and at length hatred replaces love. . . .

All these ties of love are imperfect. It is clear that limited material ties are insufficient to adequately express the universal love.

The great unselfish love for humanity is bounded by none of these imperfect, semi-selfish bonds; this is the one perfect love, possible to all mankind, and can only be achieved by the power of the Divine Spirit. No worldly power can accomplish the universal love.

NOTES

Marriage: The Bond between Husband and Wife

BAHÁ'U'LLÁH

1. *Epistle to the Son of the Wolf*, p. 49.
2. *Tablets of Bahá'u'lláh*, p. 70.
3. From a Tablet translated from the Persian, in *Women: A Compilation*, p. 22.

'ABDU'L-BAHÁ

4. *Selections from the Writings of 'Abdu'l-Bahá*, no. 86.1.
5. Ibid., no. 86.2.
6. *Bahá'í Prayers*, p. 104.
7. *Lights of Guidance*, no. 1306.
8. *Selections from the Writings of 'Abdu'l-Bahá*, no. 84.3.
9. Ibid., no. 84.4.
10. Ibid., no. 92.1.
11. *The Promulgation of Universal Peace*, p. 242.

12. Ibid., pp. 105–6.
13. Ibid., p. 253.
14. *Lights of Guidance,* no. 753.

SHOGHI EFFENDI

15. From a letter written on behalf of Shoghi Effendi to an individual, dated 15 April 1939, in *Lights of Guidance,* no. 950.
16. Ibid., dated 20 January 1943, in *Lights of Guidance,* no. 1268.
17. From a letter written on behalf of Shoghi Effendi to the National Spiritual Assembly of the United States and Canada, dated 25 October 1947, in *Lights of Guidance,* no. 1235.

THE UNIVERSAL HOUSE OF JUSTICE

18. From a letter written on behalf of the Universal House of Justice to the National Spiritual Assembly of New Zealand, dated 28 December 1980, in *The Compilation of Compilations, Vol. II,* no. 2162.
19. From a letter written on behalf of the Universal House of Justice to an individual believer, dated 3 November 1982, in *Lights of Guidance,* no. 1269.
20. From a letter of the Universal House of Justice to the Conference of the Continental Board of Counselors, dated 29 December 2015.

Children and Parenting

BAHÁ'U'LLÁH

1. From a Tablet translated from the Arabic, in
   Family Life, p. 33.

'ABDU'L-BAHÁ

2. From a talk of 'Abdu'l-Bahá, in *Lights of Guidance,* no. 733.
3. *Selections from the Writings of 'Abdu'l-Bahá,* no.
   108.1.
4. Ibid., no. 109.1.
5. Ibid., no. 110.2.
6. Ibid., no. 110.3.
7. Ibid., no. 111.8.
8. Ibid., no. 114.1.
9. *The Promulgation of Universal Peace,* p. 185.
10. *Selections from the Writings of 'Abdu'l-Bahá,* no.
    115.3.
11. Ibid., no. 122.1.
12. Ibid., no. 95.2.
13. Ibid., no. 109.1.
14. Ibid., no. 102.3.
15. Ibid., no. 103.1.
16. Ibid.
17. Ibid., no. 103.5.
18. From a Tablet translated from the Persian, in
    The Compilation of Compilations, Vol. I, no.
    590.

19. *Selections from the Writings of ʻAbdu'l-Bahá*, no. 96.2.

20. Ibid., no. 106.1.

21. From a Tablet translated from the Persian, in *The Compilation of Compilations, Vol. I*, no. 839.

22. *The Promulgation of Universal Peace*, p. 251.

23. *Selections from the Writings of ʻAbdu'l-Bahá*, no. 98.2.

24. *Some Answered Questions*, no. 62.6.

SHOGHI EFFENDI

25. From a letter written on behalf of Shoghi Effendi to an individual, dated 29 April 1933, in *The Compilation of Compilations, Vol. I*, no. 50.

THE UNIVERSAL HOUSE OF JUSTICE

26. From a letter of the Universal House of Justice to the Baháʼís of the World, Riḍván 2000.

27. Ibid.

Family Relationships

BAHÁʼUʼLLÁH

1. *Tablets of Baháʼuʼlláh*, p. 156.

2. Ibid., p. 37.

3. *Gleanings from the Writings of Baháʼuʼlláh*, no. 66.8.

4. Ibid., no. 43.4.

5. The Hidden Words, Arabic, no. 52.

6. *Gleanings from the Writings of Bahá'u'lláh,* no. 92.3.

7. Ibid., no. 72.4.

'ABDU'L-BAHÁ

8. *The Promulgation of Universal Peace,* p. 200.

9. Ibid., p. 217.

10. From a Tablet translated from the Persian, in *The Compilation of Compilations, Vol. I,* no. 860.

11. *The Promulgation of Universal Peace,* pp. 232–33.

12. Ibid., p. 232.

13. From a Tablet translated from the Persian, in *The Compilation of Compilations, Vol. I,* no. 183.

14. *The Promulgation of Universal Peace,* pp. 405–6.

15. *Selections from the Writings of 'Abdu'l-Bahá,* no. 34.2.

16. *The Promulgation of Universal Peace,* pp. 638–39.

17. Ibid., p. 639.

18. Ibid.

19. *Paris Talks,* no. 19.5.

20. *'Abdu'l-Bahá in London,* p. 91.

21. *The Promulgation of Universal Peace,* pp. 99–100.

22. Ibid., p. 100.

23. *The Secret of Divine Civilization,* ¶35.
24. *Selections from the Writings of 'Abdu'l-Bahá,* no. 35.11.
25. *Paris Talks,* no. 9.21.
26. *The Promulgation of Universal Peace,* p. 321.
27. *Selections from the Writings of 'Abdu'l-Bahá,* no. 221.9.

SHOGHI EFFENDI

28. From a letter written on behalf of Shoghi Effendi to an individual, dated 8 May 1942, in *The Compilation of Compilations, Vol. I,* no. 64.
29. From a letter written on behalf of Shoghi Effendi to an individual, dated 17 February 1933, in *Compilation on Social and Economic Development,* p. 4.

THE UNIVERSAL HOUSE OF JUSTICE

30. From a letter to the National Spiritual Assembly of the Bahá'ís of Canada, dated 19 March 1973.
31. From a letter to the National Spiritual Assembly of the Bahá'ís of New Zealand, dated 28 December 1980, in *The Compilation of Compilations, Vol. I,* no. 99.

Home

BAHÁ'U'LLÁH

1. *Tablets of Bahá'u'lláh*, p. 197.
2. The Seven Valleys, ¶73.

'ABDU'L-BAHÁ

3. From a Tablet translated from the Arabic, in
   The Compilation of Compilations, Vol. I, no.
   25.
4. *The Promulgation of Universal Peace*, p. 401.
5. Ibid., p. 5.
6. *Paris Talks*, no. 24.1.
7. *The Promulgation of Universal Peace*, pp. 103–4.
8. *'Abdu'l-Bahá in London*, p. 38.
9. *The Promulgation of Universal Peace*, p. 149.
10. From a Tablet translated from the Persian, in
    The Compilation of Compilations, Vol. I, no.
    859.

Love and Unity

BAHÁ'U'LLÁH

1. The Seven Valleys, ¶43.
2. *Tablets of Bahá'u'lláh*, p. 71.
3. *Gleanings from the Writings of Bahá'u'lláh*, no.
   132.3.
4. Ibid., no. 109.2.

5. *Selections from the Writings of 'Abdu'l-Bahá,* no. 12.1.

6. Ibid., no. 1.7.

7. *The Promulgation of Universal Peace,* p. 456.

8. Ibid., p. 128.

9. Ibid.

10. *Selections from the Writings of 'Abdu'l-Bahá,* no. 1.3.

11. Ibid., no. 221.6.

12. *Paris Talks,* no. 9.26.

13. *The Promulgation of Universal Peace,* p. 138.

14. *Paris Talks,* no. 6.7.

15. Ibid., no. 15.7.

16. Ibid., no. 41.7.

17. *Selections from the Writings of 'Abdu'l-Bahá,* no. 221.12.

18. *Paris Talks,* no. 15.8.

19. *The Promulgation of Universal Peace,* p. 477.

20. Ibid., pp. 299–300.

21. Ibid., p. 95.

22. *Selections from the Writings of 'Abdu'l-Bahá,* no. 175.5.

23. *Paris Talks,* no. 58.1.

24. Ibid., no. 58.4–7.

25. Ibid., no. 58.8.

26. Ibid., no. 1.9.

27. Ibid., no. 1.13.

28. Ibid., no. 9.1.

29. Ibid., no. 9.4.

30. Ibid., no. 9.5.
31. Ibid., no. 9.7.
32. Ibid., no. 9.8–16.

BIBLIOGRAPHY

Works of Bahá'u'lláh

The Call of the Divine Beloved: Selected Mystical Works of Bahá'u'lláh. Haifa, Israel: Bahá'í World Centre, 2018.

Epistle to the Son of the Wolf. New ed. Translated by Shoghi Effendi. 1st ps ed. Wilmette, IL: Bahá'í Publishing Trust, 1988.

Gleanings from the Writings of Bahá'u'lláh. Translated by Shoghi Effendi. Wilmette, IL: Bahá'í Publishing, 2005.

The Hidden Words. Translated by Shoghi Effendi. Wilmette, IL: Bahá'í Publishing, 2002.

Tablets of Bahá'u'lláh revealed after the Kitáb-i-Aqdas. Compiled by the Research Department of the Universal House of Justice. Translated by Habib Taherzadeh et al. Wilmette, IL: Bahá'í Publishing Trust, 1988.

Works of 'Abdu'l-Bahá

'Abdu'l-Bahá in London: Addresses & Notes of Conversations. London: Bahá'í Publishing Trust, 1987.

Paris Talks: Addresses Given By 'Abdu'l-Bahá in Paris in 1911. Wilmette, IL: Bahá'í Publishing, 2011.

Promulgation of Universal Peace: Talks Delivered by 'Abdu'l-Bahá during His Visit to the United States and Canada in 1912. Compiled by Howard MacNutt. Wilmette, IL: Bahá'í Publishing, 2012.

The Secret of Divine Civilization. Translated by Marzieh Gail and Ali-Kuli Khan. Wilmette, IL: Bahá'í Publishing, 2007.

Selections from the Writings of 'Abdu'l-Bahá. Compiled by the Research Department of the Universal House of Justice. Translated by a Committee at the Bahá'í World Center and Marzieh Gail. Wilmette, IL: Bahá'í Publishing, 2010.

Some Answered Questions. Newly translated by a Committee at the Bahá'í World Center. Haifa, Israel: Bahá'í World Centre, 2014.

Bahá'í Compilations

Bahá'í Prayers: A Selection of Prayers Revealed by Bahá'u'lláh, the Báb, and 'Abdu'l-Bahá. New ed. Wilmette, IL: Bahá'í Publishing Trust, 2002.

The Compilation of Compilations: Prepared by the Universal House of Justice, 1963–1990. 2 vols. Australia: Bahá'í Publications Australia, 1991.

Family Life: A Compilation of Extracts from the Bahá'í Writings and from Letters Written on Behalf of Shoghi Effendi and the Universal House of Justice. Wilmette, IL: Bahá'í Publishing Trust, 2008.

Lights of Guidance: A Bahá'í Reference File. Compiled by Helen Hornby. New ed. New Dehli, India: Bahá'í Publishing Trust, 1994.

Women: A Compilation, excerpts from Bahá'u'lláh, 'Abdu'l-Bahá, Shoghi Effendi and the Universal House of Justice. Compiled by the Research Department of the Universal House of Justice, 1986.